To Heather [illegible]
Best wish[illegible]
recovery, hope some of
the writings therein
bring you good tidings
and joy.
Love + Blessings,
Alan

The Doggo Book

Alan Ira Gordon

Illustrations by Marge Simon

Photos by Alan Ira Gordon

The Doggo Book
by Alan Ira Gordon

Cover photo by Alan Ira Gordon
Cover design by Laura Givens

First Printing, January 2021

Hiraeth Publishing
P.O. Box 1248
Tularosa, NM 88352

e-mail: sdpshowcase@yahoo.com

Visit www.hiraethsffh.com for science fiction, fantasy, horror, scifaiku, and more. While you are there, visit the Shop for books and more! **Support the small, independent press...**

Friend us on Facebook at Hiraeth Publish
Follow us on Twitter at @HiraethSf

Dedication

For Lucky, then, now and forever. You wrote this book with the lives that you touched and the love that you gave. I just put it down in words on paper for you.

"A dog has one aim in life. To bestow his heart."

J.R. Ackerley

"Dogs are indeed the most social, affectionate, and amiable creatures of the whole brute creation..."

Edmund Burke

"I have found that when you are deeply troubled there are things you get from the silent devoted companionship of a dog that you can get from no other source."

Doris Day

"You have a dog...be happy."

Charlie Brown

HATE HAS NO HOME HERE.

Introduction

I first heard the word "doggo" about a year ago, in one of my regular dog topic e-mail conversations with writer/editor/publisher Tyree Campbell. At the time, I assumed that it was a word that someone (Tyree, perhaps?) just made-up off-the-cuff, most likely never or rarely to be heard again.

But soon after the word kept popping-up again and again. So I just had to dig around for answers and where else to start but at Wikipedia. And therein lies the entrance to a new way of thinking about our canine friends. Wikipedia tells us that "doggo" is the key word in a whole new internet language about dogs called Dog-Speak or DoggoLingo (alternately at times referred to as woof, bork or yiff). The idea is that these new words are a dog's own idiom and are purported to be the thinking words that go on in a dog's own brain. In other words, cutesy changes to everyday words that we idiot humans assume that a dog would speak if he or she were having a conversation with a person.

While the exact origins are unknown, it all seems to have started on the internet around 2014 and taken off from there. Lots of creative people have posted memes and videos of their favorite dog pal speaking in DoggoLingo, telling us what's on their canine minds in this fun new canine twisting of familiar conversational words. Chances are you've already seen examples of DoggoLingo, its everywhere across the internet. Some common words in the lingo include *pupper* for pup, *floof* for a dog's fluffy coat and *doin' me a scare* in place of "scaring me."

My personal favorite on-line Doggo entertainment is a series of videos about "K'eyush the Stunt Husky," starring the aforementioned Siberian Husky and his British human "Mum" (also featuring Mum's Mum and their housecat or *meower*), who have wonderful conversations and arguments with K'eyush expressing his forceful opinions (as only a husky can) on everything under the sun in DoggoSpeak captions. Check-out the series, it's easily found on YouTube and Facebook.

So is this a book featuring Doggo prose? Not exactly. I wanted to title this writing collection in a manner that conveys just how wonderful it is to have dogs in all of our lives. And in that aforementioned Wikipedia page explaining DoggoLingo, I came across a quote attributed to Elyse Graham, an assistant professor at Stony Brook University, who describes DoggoLingo as "upbeat, joyful and clueless in a relentlessly friendly way."

And it struck me: that quote also describes the state of the two-way relationship between dogs and their human companions. For both parties in the *hooman-doggo* relationship, it's upbeat, joyful and, let's be honest and face it, both the dog and person are completely and mutually-clueless in their own relentlessly friendly way. Because we speak completely different languages. Which is why we invent internet languages like "DoggoSpeak" to at least imagine what's going on under our canine companions' thinking caps. And I'm pretty certain that the dogs have come-up with their own "HoomanSpeak" dialect to explain to each other what they think we're saying. They're just not telling us about it. Yet.

Thus, we're inside "The Doggo Book" right now. A fitting title for a collection of writings serving the same purpose as the made-up DoggoSpeak language: to express how wonderful it is to have our four-legged friends in our two-legged lives.

One final comment of introduction and then we're off to the Table of Contents. While I mostly write in the science fiction- fantasy genre, some of the following poems as well as the concluding real-world essay are outside of the genre. I think it would be a disservice to dogs to limit this writing effort to a narrow scope of single genre. Their hearts are so big and inviting for us to love and cherish them that a collection of dog writings should be across-the-board and wide-ranging, also.

Because to paraphrase from one of the following poems, they're so very deserved. And worth it.

Alan Ira Gordon
Worcester, Massachusetts
August, 2020

Table of Contents

The Steppenwolf Revisitation

Alan Ira Gordon

"Why did you choose to appear on a dog show?"

The question doesn't have the gravitas of Neil Armstrong's famous "one small step for man..." quote, but the moment does have the same heft in terms of world-wide historical drama. A first step of its own, to commence the aliens' first broadcast of choice for initial direct interface with the general global populace scheduled not as a news broadcast or a special show. But instead on a live version of *Dog Conversation*, the New York-based syndicated popular American television dog care show. My show.

The American and U.N. government officials provided me with a list of interview questions. I decided to lead with my own question. The Alien Leader's answer takes the interview in an unanticipated direction that transforms my given list of prepared questions into a useless scrap of paper.

"Fourteen thousand," the Alien Leader murmurs seated across from me as he gazes down toward his feet. He leans slightly forward, running his seven-fingered hand gently through the mane of my popular show co-host, my husky Lucky, who sighs contentedly.

"I beg your pardon?"

The Alien Leader doesn't rudely ignore me. He just seems politely distracted, lost somewhere else in thought.

"Fourteen thousand..." he repeats in his so soft voice. "...and yet such as him are still so close to The Original Ones."

He may be alien, but the sense of human-like wonder is clear in his voicetone. As a seasoned interviewer, I pick-up on that and run with it.

"Could you elaborate, please? I don't understand what the number means."

My question pulls the Alien Leader back from his remembrance. "I apologize. It is so amazing. After all this time...and yet some of them are so close to being the same as they were then." He gazes anew at Lucky, who sighs and wraps his canine paws tightly around my guest's stout legs.

"We expected breed divergence but not so much a concurrent line of breed stability. It is so...what is your appropriate word? Ah, yes...so Steppenwolf."

"Steppenwolf? Why do you use that term?"

"It is your word. For the original canine. The one that we introduced."

At that remark, I notice out of the corner of my eye that the studio staff halts their various work tasks and stare.

"Introduced," I reply. "Are you telling me that you actually brought dogs to Earth?"

My guest finally gives me his full attention, pulling away from the dozing Lucky to look directly at me. He knows that we're heading directly into it, now.

"Yes. I led that expedition, also."

The number makes sense to me, now. "Fourteen thousand. You mean years ago. That's the historic time period when dogs were first noticed by humankind and initially domesticated. And you led..." My voice trails off under the sheer weight of all those years.

"Given the laws of relativity for interstellar travel, it was not that long ago for our expedition. But long enough. A beginning to The Test."

The studio staff stirs and whispers anew with that statement, prompting me to another question. "Test? What kind of test?"

"Interspecies bonding, of course. The dogs of my world bonded into a dual species with my people, similar to your race's situation today. Upon discovering your planet and race, we applied the experiment." He strokes Lucky's head while still gazing directly at me. "And the outcome was similar to us. See how your two species have bonded into a symbiotic co-existence as we had hoped."

"And why did you hope for this result?"

Lucky sits-up and rests his chin on the Alien Leader's massive knee, then closes his eyes anew in response to continued petting.

"We needed a unit of measurement to determine whether humankind had the capacity to evolve. Not technologically, but empathetically. Your EQ ability, so to speak. Our homeworld experience reflected our own ability to merge into a sociological bonding with dogs as an indicator of such. So we have conducted this experiment on many worlds. Some species fail to bond with our partners. Others succeed very well. As you did here on Earth."

I have spent a lifetime conducting interviews and have learned that many answers easily produce further questions for me to ask. One immediately springs to mind.

"But why go through all the effort of this test? Why does any of this matter?"

It's as if Lucky also wonders, as he opens his cobalt-blue eyes and gazes-up at our guest.

"To determine your worthiness. If you can develop such a loving bond with the canine species, evolve to love and depend so much upon each other, then you are ready. To enter into the same caring and considerate bond with those of us in the interstellar community."

We sit in silence for a moment as the implication of the invitation sinks in. Then once again the professional interviewer in me takes over.

"So this is what you've been speaking to our government about since your arrival."

"No. It is what I have come to speak to you about."

"Directly to the public on this show?"

"No. You asked why I chose to appear on your show. I came to see you."

"Me."

"We need to designate Earth's Ambassador. One to represent your people to the interstellar community. And we wish that person to be you. An individual most skilled in assisting to maintain the canine-human relationship will bring that ability to establishing and maintaining the Earth-interstellar relationship."

I don't need to ponder my answer.

"No."

The Alien Leader's face takes-on a familiar look of surprise.

"No?"

"I'm afraid not."

"But why?"

"My reason is right in front of you." I gesture at Lucky. "You did well in pairing our species. I can't...I won't leave him. We need each other."

The Alien Leader reacts by standing-up, now towering-over me to his full seven-foot height. He takes a breath and emits a sound the likes of which have never been heard on Earth prior to his expedition's recent arrival. A sound which has been broadcast on television of late and explained as his specie's form of laughter.

"My new friend. You misunderstand. The canine species is the glue, so to speak, that holds together the many races and worlds of the interstellar community. We have evolved our alliance's sense of love, empathy and respect for each other from that original bond which first developed with our dog partners. We would never dream of separating you two."

"You mean-"

"Yes. We want you both as our co-ambassadors."

As if he understands my guest's words, Lucky stands and trots over to sit by my side, leaning into my knee. Ready to serve. I reach down and rub the thick husky fur of his neck.

"Then I...we accept."

"Good." The Alien Leader turns and gestures to one of his crewmembers off-camera stationed at the studio door. He responds by opening the door, through which yet another crewman emerges alongside a large, friendly-looking husky. A husky that for all intents and purposes looks mostly like Lucky, yet minutely different. Slightly alien.

The dog trots over to us and both Earth-native and Off-world huskies quickly take to each other, as meeting dogs usually do. A few moments pass and the Alien Leader speaks anew.

"May we leave now? We have much to discuss in preparation for our newfound relationship."

As the four of us leave the studio together, a thought occurs. "What's your dog's name?"

The Alien leader replies in his native tongue. I ask what it translates as.

"The name does not translate exactly. I suppose the closest connotation would be your term 'brings good fortune.'"

"So...Lucky."

"Why, yes. I do suppose so."

"Funny," I reply. "How so many dog people coincidentally end-up giving their dogs the same name."

The Alien Leader looks momentarily startled by this comment. Then he repeats that earlier sound of laughter never before heard on Earth. A sound that Lucky and I look forward to hearing often during our newfound adventure to the stars.

First Contact

We were so delighted to see
peering-out at us through the landed
spaceship portals, the familiar
of happy, beaming canine faces.

And even more surprised when
we soon after saw those same canine
faces behind the helmet visors
of the emerging alien crew.

SIMON

Lucky and His Dad

On full-moon nights, The Rainbow
Bridge becomes a two-way street
and Lucky's back; on those nights
through my front window I'd see his
Siberian Husky spectral self reunited
with my neighbor old Bob on their
usual routine of a midnight walk.

Last month, Bob himself finally
passed so I figured that's the end
of that. But by the light of tonight's
full moon, darned if there's not
the two of 'em, a spectral pair together
making their midnight rounds.

It's a comfort, actually, proof
positive that eventually I'll be reunited
over that Rainbow Bridge with my
own snow dog boys. I think sometime
we'll join Lucky and Bob on one of
their full-moon walks. It'll be good
to be back in the old neighborhood.

Venus in the Southeast Sky

No UFO in soft approach
From out the evening sky

No mythic beast in wooded shade
Ahiss toward clawed attack

No nameless slither underfoot
Intent on ankle grab

No shapeless lurk from neighbor's side
O'er top the backyard fence

No rising yawp nor fearsome growl
Sustained amidst deep dark

Yet silence as Sweet Dog and I
Give Thanks our nighttime world.

Dog Love

Love you beyond belief,
every single day beyond
what words can describe,
but I have to try putting
it in words every day,
because you're so very deserved.
And worth it.

Dog Photo

One dog photo framed
and hung on the wall
is worth a thousand
digital images stored
in The Cloud.

Dog Poem No. 1

Any day with you
is the best day
of my life.

When the Aliens Arrived on Earth to Visit the Dogs

They spent many a summer
afternoon spread-out
in places like Muncie
Jakarta and Saint Petersburg.
As well as off-the-beaten-paths
in African veldt villages,
dusty Cairo back alleyways
and by the occasional
Burger King dumpster.

Ignoring all human entreaties,
from media camera crews
to average citizen outreach
and government delegations.

With long, tapering ET-like fingers
they stroked each canine mane,
lovingly petted all brows
and provided water
along with locally-purchased
kibbles and treats.

All the while whispering
into canine ears
a steady stream of instruction,
commentary or just plain praise
it was hard to tell.

The dogs nodded knowingly,
from time-to-time replying
with a soft ruff
or brief vocalization.

At summer's end, they departed
as abruptly as they'd arrived.
The dogs stood and watched
them go.

As the wind of starship wakes
died down, each dog
licked respective chops,
circled in ritual no more than

ten times each,
and plopped back down for
a late afternoon nap.

As if the summertime
events had never occurred.

Anthropomorphism 101

My dog sees buses
as serene tusked elephants
aglide worn pathway city streets,
majestic lords of all that they perceive.

Garbage and recycling trucks are
truculent hippos, grumping and snuffling
curbside as they nose about for household
waste stream treats.

Early morning skittished joggers
topped legs like piping plovers lean
stride swiftly midst our walking route,
tempting my boy as running meats.

How must they view, mine pup and I,
those metaphoric untamed beasts
as master/pet, companion each,
perhaps ourselves twin morphic feasts.

So do take care each sunshined morn
astride with pup the city streets,
one never knows how might be seen
by those who hold creative keen.

Schrodinger's Pup

It doesn't matter whether
or not the box has been
opened or remains closed.
There is no conjecture
or need for a theoretical
physics calculation, proof
or theorem to get involved.

The simple matter is this:
If there's a pup-in-the-box
(and assuming for the purpose
of this discussion that there is),
then there's only one possible
outcome and one outcome only.
No other possibilities at all.

He...or well, maybe She (I'll give
you that for the one possible
derivation)...He or She is definitely
alive and alert and ready-to-eat (always
ready to eat!) and energetic
and rambunctious and handsome/
beautiful and smart and a character,
yes, quite a character!

And of course loving. Unconditionally
loving. That goes without saying.

So, on second thought.
Why waste any time at all with
the pup-in-a-box experiment?

Just do the cat thing with the box
instead.

And just love the dog.
As He or She will love you back.
With certainty. Complete across-
the-multi-verse certainty.
And joy.

Doggo Relatives, Of Various Sorts

Werewolf Eating Disorder

I only eat the big toes.
Oh, and the occasional earlobe,
I do loves me some occasional earlobe!
I'm basically the family scandal
Dad shakes his graying mane
and lectures me about the waste
of a good rest-of-a-kill.

But look at it this way:
It's not like back-in-the-day,
when folks took better care
of themselves.
Given all of the toxic junk
that people eat these days,
I'm actually better-off
limiting my diet to the select
edge bits-and-pieces.

And hey, it's not like I'm the first
picky eater in the family.
I could be a worse culinary embarrassment,
along the lines of old Uncle Max.
Let's face it...he earned
his nickname
of Ass Man.

Signs of the Zombie Pet Apocalypse

The dogs.
All they want us to do
is pet them. Endlessly,
mindlessly and ceaselessly.
Pet them.

And the cats.
Nothing has changed.
They're still aloof
and completely ignoring
us.

Guess that even during The End
Of Days, at heart I'm still
a dog person.

Wolf Alice

Cunning and betrayal in such
a pretty package...the unsuspecting
wolf took-in the waif
of a lost and feral child,
bestowing kindness and unconditional
love, for which she was known
throughout the fabled land.

Years of sacrifice to the bone
paid for the child's education, fostering
a natural writing talent
through grade school then college,
blooming into a literary career.

And the payback for the decades
of wolfen maternal sacrifice?
A vengeful re-writing of the true
cross-species nurturing, a twisting
from faithful goodness into a dark fabling
of supposed carnivorous threats, dangers
and just plain badness (the better
to eat you, *my dear*!),
cascading down the ages
as a permanent alternative fact.

As it was said...cunning and betrayal
in such a pretty package,
such was Wolf Alice, for the child
may be taken from the dark
woods, yet the dark woods
cannot be taken out of
the child.

Cybernetic Doggos

Still require daily walks,
with oil discharges spotting
neighborhood lawns and streets.

Vampire Doggos

Are turning the tide:
One quick night-time walk nip
and each victim joins the expanding
ranks of dog lovers;
cats' days of household
living ease
are numbered.

Now Back To Doggos

Canine Occam's Razor

Why do we love
dogs so much?

And why do dogs love
us back with such always
undeniable one-hundred-and
-one percent unconditional
love?

It's simple. It's just because
they're such great guys.
Such great, great guys.
Easy answer.
Case closed.

SIMON

The Inter-Galactic Legend of the Canine

Academics and researchers across
the galaxy find it as a commonality
amongst so many worlds
and civilizations; a shared ancient
legend of a creature, four-legged
and furred of one species, yet
many distinct breeds, from tiny
in size to huge, with various
styles and personalities.

The legend differs in detail
from world-to-world yet shares
a singular trait: the mythical
creature is revered for one unique
characteristic.

A self-less and unconditional
love for the sentient companion
species of its homeworld, like
none seen amongst companion species
of any other world.

Some cultures say that this wondrous
creature and its companion species
exist to this day, on a small, obscure
blue-green world in a quiet and distant
pocket of known space.

Yet most experts of inter-planetary
myth concur that the tale is just
that: a hopeful, even wishful tale.
For no creature in reality could be
so giving, loyal and unconditionally
loving to another. And no one singular
world and race could be so lucky,
so fortunate to be blessed with such
a wonderful companion species.

Or could it?

Pocket Universe #36- Superhero Canine Sidekicks

In this alternative multi-verse place
and time, the superheroes' practice
is to each team-up with a canine
sidekick for all activities pertaining
to *Truth, Justice and The American Way.*

Batman started it all off with Barry,
his loyal and equally stoic American Bulldog.

Wonder Woman flew her invisible
plane paired-up with Winnie,
a husky-shepherd mix with the most
fashionable cobalt blue eyes.

Over in the Marvel Group, Iron
Man made the action scene side-kicked
with Rusty, a scrappy mutt decked-out
in his own doggo iron suit.

Everyone's favorite neighborhood Spider-Man
web-slung through The Big Apple
with Little Petey riding shotgun in
his specially-designed Spidey
chest harness.

The Justice League was side-kicked
by Snapper, a feisty big-ego Chihuahua
who was convinced he was in charge
of the team (they let him think so).

I could go on-and-on through the rest
of the superhero-verse, calling-out
Green Arrow and Sharpie,
Black Canary and Midge,
Captain America and Bow-Wow-Bucky,
etc., etc., etc.
You get the picture.

But what about The Big Man
Himself? Superman always blazed
his own original and unique trail,
going his own way. And side-
kicking was no exception.

He took-out a Help Wanted ad
in *The Daily Planet*, then thoroughly
and professionally interviewed
and tested applicants, finally settling
on a human partner. A guy from
out-of-town named Karl. Together
they fought crime and super-villains by
night while selling insurance by day.

But as Fate would have it, eventually
Karl was offed as the duo battled
one of Lex Luthor's grand schemes.
And soon after, a grief-stricken hero
learned something he hadn't known
about his late partner: Karl had an unexpected
civilian life sidekick of his own, a cute
pup named Krypto.

So our Hero took little Krypto home and kept him. Not to train as a crime-fighting partner. But instead to share a Forever Home. Just Clark Kent and Krypto, together enjoying park walks, doggo-friend playdates and games of fetch at the beach.

A special team in their own way, for sure. And they couldn't ask for a more super team-up than that.

You Adapt

You adapt when you bring home
your puppy. You adapt by waking-
up earlier for morning walks,
puppy-proofing the house in so
many ways. Non-slip throw rugs
over hardwood floors, chew toys
and rawhides and treats for training
and good behavior.

You adapt as your puppy grows
into young adulthood, strong and lean
making the fenced-in backyard his own
personal kingdom. You adapt to long,
strong walks and hikes as he chooses
for each journey from amongst
his multiple routes, his harnessed
back muscles rippling in front of you
beneath beautiful fur, gliding effortlessly
over concrete sidewalks, granite curbing,
roadways and open spaces.

You adapt to his middle-aged years, when
he still maintains youthfulness but is no longer
growing, plateaued into his habits
and behaviors. You take comfort in
your mutual routines, the walks and trips
and games, knowing each other's likes
and dislikes, cuddle styles and personal
tics that make both of you who you are
together.

You can't imagine living any other way.
You adapt as the years flow by and one
day you realize that you're together in
his senior years. You adapt to him moving
slower now, still intent on your mutual
routines but at a quieter pace, the distances
shorter, the times briefer, the routines
that he now chooses to occasionally skip.

You adapt to the senior dog health issues.
The advancing ailments and growing
list of medications, more frequent trips
to the vet (both scheduled and emergency),
the challenges of special diets, therapies
and treatments.

You adapt to the growing mountain
of it all, for it's all so very worth it,
as sandwiched in between the stress
and the fear and the discomfort is
the familiar of walks and games
and the simple pure moments of
your mutual lifetime of continuous
joy together.

You adapt to it getting harder,
to knowing that it's coming to
an end. Knowing that you can't stop
it from its unscheduled arrival.
You adapt to it breathing on your neck
while you do your best to focus on
his needs, keeping him happy and
comfortable and secure within your
well-worn and cherished routines.

And you adapt to a growing sense
that he knows it too and in his own
way, he's cooperating and working
with you on all of the minute-to-
minute challenges of it all.

As you adapt together.

And then you don't adapt.

You don't adapt to the aftermath
of whichever one of the oh-so-many
ways from which you choose to take
your parting. You don't adapt to
the indescribable sense of loss,
your new reality of incompleteness,
knowing that he's not suffering and
in a better rainbowed place but
it's not enough as you plod minute-
after-minute, hour-after-hour, day-
after-day through the emptiness.

And you wait for the grief and pain
and emptiness to leave but it doesn't.
And sooner or later you come to
realize that it will never go away,
it's now a part of who you are, basic
to your very being. The love
and the good are inseparable
from the pain and the loss,
permanent within your being.
As is he.

And you embrace all of that, accept
it as the God-given gift that he was,
still is, and forever will be.
And you decide to honor him.
By adapting yet again.

You adapt by bringing your new
puppy home. You adapt by making room
in your heart side-by-side for both
of them, not a replacement but
a co-existence, a continuance by which
the loss is transformed into the ultimate
gift, a joining within you of one canine
companion to the next. The three of
you in the continuum of life.
Together.

A wondrous continuing life of love.

For Sam.
For Beau.
And most of all for Lucky.
Loving you all forever together
in my heart.

Essay

My Husky Angel Lucky

Alan Ira Gordon

At 9 months old, my sweet husky boy Lucky came into my life. He was aptly named, as I often told people that he was lucky to have me and I was just as lucky to have him. It felt very natural to nickname him Angel, as he had both the sweetest angelic smile and personality of anyone, person or dog, you'd ever meet. So every morning when we woke-up I would greet him by saying "good morning, angel."

Long walks and hikes are mandatory for a snow dog husky, but I quickly realized that he also needed his very own outdoor kingdom to preside over. So within a few months, I hired a contractor to clear trees and brush, doubling the size of the backyard, while another contractor installed a six-foot high white vinyl fence with three gates along the periphery of the large backyard.

Lucky now had his own kingdom to preside over. We had a lot of fun together in the backyard playing with dog toys, running around and enjoying Lucky's wading pool in the summertime. But Lucky loved two particular things the most. One was resting in the shade under the lone, large pine tree located in the back center of the yard. He picked one particular spot under the tree as his favorite.

His other favorite backyard activity was playing with soccer balls. As he matured, Lucky grew to be unusually large for a husky, long and tall and topping-out at 102 pounds. He could easily grasp a soccer ball in his mouth and loved for the two of us to play throwing the ball and bringing it back to me. Over time, Lucky's soccer ball collection grew to a total of six along with one favorite tennis ball thrown-in for good measure. And of course, he had his particular favorite soccer ball, originally a bright green but eventually chewed and worn beyond its original features.

The years passed, filled with fun and adventures along with the expected ups-and-downs of life. Lucky made sure that for both of us, the good always outweighed the more challenging times. At age 10, Lucky began to slow a bit but was still hale and hearty. Then in December of his 11th year, my angel Lucky was diagnosed with diabetes. Life became more complicated for us both, as medication needs grew and our world of long walks steadily shortened, shrinking-down to spending time in Lucky's beloved backyard. Although his world became limited, Lucky was still the happiest guy I knew, human or canine, just enjoying the afternoon sun in his favorite spot beneath his backyard pine tree.

The inevitable time came on a perfectly sunny July afternoon and Lucky left me to cross over The Rainbow Bridge. Although I understood that it was his time to go be with God, being without Lucky after 12 years together was very hard. I knew that my grief would ease over time, but some days were just worse than others. The backyard was unbearably empty without Lucky presiding over his kingdom. I left his six soccer balls and the tennis balls where they always were, in a circle on the lawn by the sundeck close to the house.

About a month after Lucky has passed on, I had a few better days. Then suddenly grief once again overwhelmed me and I had a terrible night, feeling his loss as deeply as I had on the day that he left. It was a difficult and sleepless night.

In the kitchen early the next morning, I raised the window blinds and looked directly out into the backyard. I immediately noticed a difference. Lucky's favorite soccer ball was no longer with the rest of them near the sundeck but was all by itself way deep in the back of the yard. It was resting alone in Lucky's favorite spot under his pine tree.

I went out into the backyard and thought about it. There had been no wind overnight to move the ball. Plus all of the other balls hadn't moved at all. Even if a small animal had crawled under the fence and moved it, that had never, ever happened before. In 12 years. And it was Lucky's very favorite ball. Now resting for the first time ever very far away from the rest of the balls near the house. Under his pine tree in his favorite spot.

And I knew for sure. In my darkest hour, my angel Lucky had sent me a sign, a message that he was o.k. over The Rainbow Bridge. And I knew that with Lucky still watching over me and loving me, that I would be o.k., too.

A Bibliography of Enjoyable Books on Various Doggo Subjects:

Cold Noses and Warm Hearts by Laurie Morrow, Willow Creek Press, 1996

Conversations With My Dog by Zig Zigler, Broadman & Holman Publishers, 2005

Dog Quotations by Helen Exley, Hallmark Books, 1993

E.B. White on Dogs edited by Martha White, Tilbury House Publishers, 2013

First Dogs-American Presidents and Their Best Friends by Roy Rowan & Brooke Janis, Algonquin Books of Chapel Hill, 1997

How Dogs Think: What the World Looks Like to Them and Why They Act the Way They Do by Stanley Coren, Simon & Schuster, Inc., 2004

Inside Of A Dog: What Dogs See, Smell And Know by Alexandra Horowitz, Scribner, 2009

Mutts (Volume 6)-A Little Look-See by Patrick McDonnell, Andrews McMeel Publishing, 2001

Rin Tin Tin-The Life And The Legend by Susan Orlean, Simon & Shuster, 2011

Snoopy's Guide to the Writing Life edited by Barnaby Conrad and Monte Schulz, Writer's Digest Books, 2002

The Art Of Racing In The Rain by Garth Stein, Harper, 2008

The Dog Who Loved Too Much-Tales, Treatments and the Psychology of Dogs by Dr. Nicholas Dodman, Bantam Books, 1996

The Intelligence of Dogs-Canine Consciousness and Capabilities by Stanley Coren, The Free Press, 1994

The World of Dogs, forward by Barbara Woodhouse, Chartwell Books Inc., 1974.

Thunder Dog-The True Story of A Blind Man, His Guide Dog & the Triumph of Trust at Ground Zero by Michael Hingson with Susy Flory, Thomas Nelson Publishing, 2011

Throw The Damn Ball-Classic Poetry By Dogs by R.D. Rosen, Harry Prichett and Rob Battles, Penguin Books, 2013

Ultimate Dog Care-A Complete Veterinary Guide by Sue Guthrie, Dick Lane and Professor Geoffrey Sumner-Smith, Howell Book House, 2001

101 Salivations-For The Love Of Dogs by Rachael Hale, Bulfinch Press, 2003

Canine Chronicles by Angel Favazza, Alban Lake Publishing, 2014

The following poems and stories included in this collection were previously published in the following periodicals:

<u>Dog Eyes Magazine</u>

The Steppenwolf Revisitation*

<u>Illumen</u>

Anthropomorphism 101
First Contact (2020)
Lucky and His Dad (2020)**

<u>Planet Hunter</u>

Venus In The Southeast Sky (2018)
Werewolf Eating Disorder (2018)
Wolf Alice (2018)

<u>Star*Line Magazine</u>

When The Aliens Arrived On Earth To Visit The Dogs (2017)

*Reprinted in Outposts Of Beyond (2018)

**Reprinted in Shelter of Daylight (2020)

Alan Ira Gordon is an urban planning professor at Worcester State University and writer of science fiction/fantasy poetry and short stories. His fiction has been published in various magazines including Starshore Magazine, Worcester Magazine, Disturbed Digest, Dog Eyes Magazine, Outposts Of Beyond and The Martian Wave, as well as various short story anthologies. His poetry publications include Analog Magazine and The Magazine of Fantasy & Science Fiction and he's a frequent contributor to Star*Line, the quarterly journal of the Science Fiction & Fantasy Poetry Association (SFPA).

Alan's science fiction/fantasy poetry has received five Rhysling Award nominations, a Dwarf Star Award nomination and an Analog Magazine year's best nomination (Second Place Award). His 2019 poetry collection Planet Hunter was nominated for the SFPA Elgin Award. Alan guest-edited Issue #24 of Eye To The Telescope, the on-line publication of the Science Fiction & Fantasy Poetry Association (SFPA). His poetry, short stories and articles have been published in various genre magazines and anthologies, a partial list of which can be found on his website at www.alaniragordon.com.

CPSIA information can be obtained
at www.ICGtesting.com
Printed in the USA
JSHW021936200221
11878JS00005BA/61